AF228529

BABY HORSES

by Martha London

Cody Koala

An Imprint of Pop!
popbooksonline.com

abdobooks.com

Published by Pop!, a division of ABDO, PO Box 398166, Minneapolis, Minnesota 55439. Copyright © 2021 by POP, LLC. International copyrights reserved in all countries. No part of this book may be reproduced in any form without written permission from the publisher. Pop!™ is a trademark and logo of POP, LLC.

Printed in the United States of America, North Mankato, Minnesota

052020
092020

THIS BOOK CONTAINS RECYCLED MATERIALS

Cover Photo: iStockphoto
Interior Photos: iStockphoto, 1; Shutterstock Images, 5 (top), 5 (bottom left), 5 (bottom right), 6, 9, 10, 13 (top), 13 (bottom left), 13 (bottom right), 14, 17, 19, 20–21

Editor: Nick Rebman
Series Designer: Christine Ha

Library of Congress Control Number: 2019954950
Publisher's Cataloging-in-Publication Data

Names: London, Martha, author.
Title: Baby horses / by Martha London
Description: Minneapolis, Minnesota : POP!, 2021 | Series: Baby farm animals | Includes online resources and index
Identifiers: ISBN 9781532167454 (lib. bdg.) | ISBN 9781532168550 (ebook)
Subjects: LCSH: Horses--Infancy--Juvenile literature. | Foals--Juvenile literature. | Baby horses--Juvenile literature. | Baby farm animals--Juvenile literature. | Animal babies--Juvenile literature.
Classification: DDC 636.1--dc23

Cody Koala

Pop open this book and you'll find QR codes like this one, loaded with information, so you can learn even more!

Scan this code* and others like it while you read, or visit the website below to make this book pop.

popbooksonline.com/baby-horses

*Scanning QR codes requires a web-enabled smart device with a QR code reader app and a camera.

Table of Contents

Chapter 1

A Bed of Straw

Baby horses are called foals. Foals are **mammals**. Many foals are born in barns. Each **stall** is filled with soft straw. Straw keeps the foals warm.

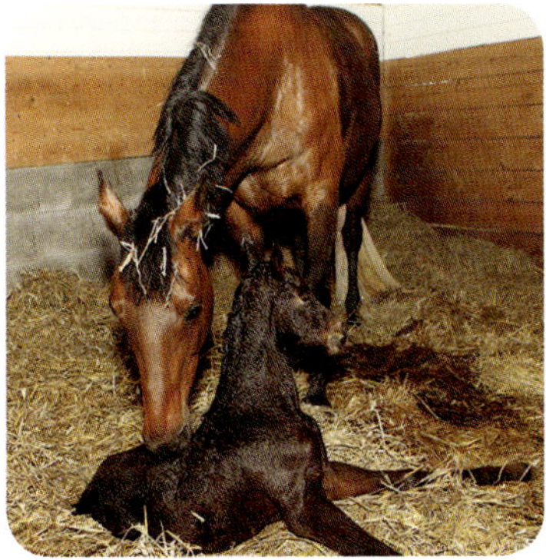

Watch a video here!

Foals can stand and walk shortly after they are born. They can run when they are one day old. Foals stay close to their mothers. Mothers protect their foals. They call to the foals if they go too far away.

Long Legs, Long Tail

Foals have long legs. The long legs help foals run fast. They can keep up with older horses. Foals' feet are covered by **hooves**.

A foal's legs do not get much longer as the animal grows up.

Learn more here!

ear
tail
nose
leg
hoof

A foal's tail is covered with long hair. The tail helps swat bugs. It also shows how the foal is feeling. A lowered tail can mean the horse is afraid. A raised tail can mean the horse is happy.

Chapter 3

Growing Up

A foal drinks its mother's milk. Over time, it begins to eat grass too. When a foal is five or six months old, farmers separate it from its mother. This is called **weaning**.

Learn more here!

Farmers wean groups of foals together. They put all the foals in the same field. That way, foals do not get lonely. The foals learn how to live apart from their mothers. Foals learn to eat only grass and grain.

After one year, a foal becomes a yearling. But it is not yet an adult. Young horses keep growing for a few more years. Most horses are fully grown by the time they are five years old.

A young female horse is called a filly. A young male horse is called a colt.

Chapter 4

Part of a Herd

Horses are **social**. They live in groups. Groups of horses are called **herds**. Some people keep horses as pets. They train and ride their horses.

Complete an
activity here!

Some horses have jobs.
For example, some police
officers ride horses. Other
people use horses to pull

carts. Some people also use horses to help with farming. Horses can pull plows and other farm equipment.

Making Connections

Text-to-Self

Would you want to ride a horse? Describe what it might be like.

Text-to-Text

Have you read books about other mammals? How are horses similar to and different from those animals?

Text-to-World

Why do you think some police officers use horses instead of cars?

Glossary

herd – a large group of animals that live and travel together.

hooves – the hard parts that cover an animal's feet.

mammal – a type of animal that has hair or fur and feeds milk to its young.

social – enjoying the company of others.

stall – a room in a barn that holds an animal.

wean – to teach an animal to eat food that is not its mother's milk.

Index

herds, 18

hooves, 8, 10

jobs, 20

legs, 8, 10

milk, 12

tail, 10, 11

weaning, 12, 15

yearling, 16

Online Resources

popbooksonline.com

Thanks for reading this Cody Koala book!

Scan this code* and others like it in this book, or visit the website below to make this book pop!

popbooksonline.com/baby-horses

*Scanning QR codes requires a web-enabled smart device with a QR code reader app and a camera.